PAPIER MÂCHÉ
·STYLE·

ALEX MacCORMICK

Photographs by
MICHAEL HARVEY

PAPIER MÂCHÉ STYLE

■ *100 step-by-step designs*

MICHAEL O'MARA BOOKS LIMITED

For my brother and sister,
Neil MacCormick and Fionna Cardale,
with love.

First published in 1994 by Michael O'Mara Books Ltd,
9 Lion Yard, Tremadoc Road, London SW4 7NQ

Text copyright © 1994 by Michael O'Mara Books Ltd
Photographs copyright © 1994 by Michael Harvey

A CIP catalogue record for this book is available from the
British Library

ISBN 1-85479-912-6 (hardback)
ISBN 1-85479-710-7 (paperback)

Edited by Veronica Sperling
Designed by Yvonne Dedman
Technical advice by Amanda Godden
Typeset by Florencetype Ltd, Kewstoke, Avon
Printed and bound in Germany by Graphischer Großbetrieb
Pößneck GmbH
A member of the Mohndruck printing group

10 9 8 7 6 5 4 3 2 1

ACKNOWLEDGEMENTS

The author and publishers would like to thank the following
for their generous help:

All the gifted artists listed on page 127 who made and
loaned their work to be photographed for this book; photog-
rapher Michael Harvey and assistant Jeremy Murch for fun
and expertise in the studio; Amanda Godden, our technical
adviser, who also made most of the papier mâché pieces in
the Basic Techniques section; Melanie Williams for making
the chickenwire pigs for the section on Basic Techniques;
Sybilla Lewyska and Bridget Garrett for painting backgrounds
and bases; Valerie Wade Antiques, 108 Fulham Road, London
SW3 6HS, for the illustration on p. 6 and for the loan of the
box on p. 8; Sarah Beales of Nomad Art, 791 Fulham Road,
London SW6, Davina Instone of Crocodile Leap, 15 Bellevue
Road, London SW17 7EG, and Sally Bryant of 7 + 7 Interiors,
91 Northcote Road, London SW11 6PL, for the loan of papier
mâché pieces by various makers.

Finally, the author would like to thank editors David
Roberts and Alison Bell, and copy-editor Veronica Sperling.

**Half-title page: Bowls
(Carol Hill)**

**Title page: Vases and
bowls (Maureen Hamilton-
Hill)**

**Contents page: Handmade
sheet (Carol Hill)**

·CONTENTS·

·INTRODUCTION·

Papier mâché invites imaginative experiment – there are no unbreakable rules, no restrictions, no prescribed traditions. It may look like metal, wood or porcelain, yet, when you pick up even a large paper object, it is always surprisingly light. Papier mâché has a certain magical allure few can resist: rather like an alchemist turning base metal into gold, you can transform mundane ingredients into beautiful and useful objects.

Over the last few years there has been a tremendous revival of interest in this artistic craft, and its creative possibilities are once more being recognized. The appeal of papier mâché rests on three main factors. Firstly, it is great fun because it is easy to make, and is both soothing and inspiring to work with. Secondly, this is a very versatile medium, which can be used to shape anything from a dinosaur or a giant sculpture, through furnishings such as chairs, clocks, cupboards, mirror frames and lamps to delicate jewelry, dolls, vases, masks and chess pieces. Thirdly, the basic materials required are inexpensive and readily available, often in your own home – newspapers, string and surplus cardboard packaging, for instance.

The opportunity to recycle materials is particularly appealing to those who care about conservation and do not have money to throw away. This was also the case in centuries past.

Although it is widely believed that the name 'papier mâché' comes from the French words *papier* (paper) and *mâcher* (to chew), recent research indicates that the term most likely derives from the English verb 'to mash' or mix with water and the pronunciation of the words was simply garbled over the years. No matter what the correct derivation, people have taken the trouble to conserve and recycle paper ever since it was first invented in China, it is said, early in the second century AD.

The skills developed by the Chinese in moulding such articles as warriors' helmets and pots from papier mâché hardened with lacquer gradually spread along the routes of traders and warring armies eastward to Japan and Korea, and westward in the eighth century via Samarkand to Damascus in what is now Syria.

Once the Arabs learned how to recycle waste material, including valuable paper, the techniques were slowly disseminated as far afield as Morocco in North Africa.

By the eleventh century such knowledge extended into Europe through France and Spain. However, it appears that the Italians learned the craft by a more direct route – from Venetian merchants who traded in the Far East – and, in turn, the Italians taught craftsmen in Persia and India how to decorate papier mâché in the Florentine style with flowers and foliage. Such designs are still commonly seen today on objects made in Kashmir and elsewhere in the sub-continent.

In the East, where lacquering and decorating papier mâché became a highly prized art form, pieces were for centuries only made to order for aristocratic patrons and so were not available for export. It was not until the sixteenth century, therefore, that the first examples of such work were brought to Europe by Portuguese merchants and, later, by Dutchmen, from whom English travellers purchased cabinets and screens to take home. In 1600 the English East India Company set up trade links with Japan, China and India, and within fifteen years its first ship returned laden with Japanese 'scritoires [desks], trunks, beoubes [screens], cups and dishes of all sorts and of a most excellent varnish'.

It was this 'most excellent varnish', highly polished and hard wearing, as well as the beautifully painted decoration beneath, which excited the interest of European collectors and eventually makers alike. The resin of trees indigenous to the Far East which formed the lacquer was difficult to duplicate in the West and so it was not until late in the seventeenth century that European makers met with much success in what became known as 'japanning'. In the meantime, the rarity and cost of imported oriental black lacquer ware – generally termed 'Japan ware' no matter whether it came from China, Japan or India – had created a fashionable market in which demand far exceeded supply.

To meet this need workshops and, later, factories were set up in various countries including France, Britain, Germany and Russia. Many major innovations originated in France, where in the mid-eighteenth century papier mâché was used to imitate plaster and stucco decorations on ceilings and walls, and to form objets d'art and furniture. French influence swiftly crossed the borders to other countries, in particular Germany,

◀ **A selection of antique papier mâché (Valerie Wade)**

which in the 1800s became famous for its sophisticated papier mâché dolls' heads, and to England, where the greatest scale of production was achieved.

Between 1770 and 1870 the craft was at its peak in terms of artistry, production and sales. Birmingham and Wolverhampton in the British Midlands became the prime centres. In 1788 one Charles Ducrest was granted a patent for 'making paper for the building of houses, bridges, ships, boats and all sorts of wheel carriages, sedan chairs, tables and book cases, either entirely of paper, or wood and iron covered in paper'. The range of products made from papier mâché increased considerably and by 1850 it was said that 'few houses can now be found in which some useful and elegant trifle may not be seen made of this exquisite material'.

From Britain and other European countries both goods and expertise were transmitted to the USA, where in 1850 the Litchfield Manufacturing Company set up the first factory for lacquered papier mâché in Litchfield, Connecticut. There followed the foundation of several other factories, in Connecticut and in Boston, Mass. In the late 1890s an Act of Congress even permitted the maceration of withdrawn banknotes to create commercial pulp – which was then moulded into replicas of national monuments and busts of eminent Americans. Nowadays these mottled grey ornaments are collectors' items.

By 1920 public tastes had changed and the last manufacturer of papier mâché in England had ceased trading. Until recently this remarkable craft was largely forgotten in the West, except in those few schools where young children were encouraged to struggle with gluey fingers over lumpen dishes and animals. Now, nearly 1800 years after paper was first invented, we are able to participate in the exciting renaissance of papier mâché.

In the following twenty-nine pages practical advice is offered on the basic materials, equipment and techniques used by craftspeople today. Do, please, spare the time to read these sections before launching into your first project if you wish to achieve the most satisfactory results. On the subsequent eighty-nine pages you will find invaluable guidance and stunning illustrations of some of the myriad ways in which you, like the makers whose work is shown in this book, can create your own Papier Mâché Style.

◄ **Kashmiri box, 1869**
(Valerie Wade)

BASIC EQUIPMENT ·AND MATERIALS·

You will find that most of the materials and equipment required for creating papier mâché objects are readily available in your own home or from local craft/art supplies shops. This list illustrates some of the basic requirements; a few more specialized ingredients are listed, where appropriate, at the start of a project.

■ WORK SURFACE

You need a large flat area where work can be left undisturbed. Cover the surface in plastic sheeting or with opened out supermarket plastic carrier bags to protect the work top and prevent objects from sticking to it.

■ PAPER

Newspapers – broadsheets are better quality paper than tabloids; pink plus white ones are useful for distinguishing layers; tear into pieces, never cut with scissors.

Wall-lining paper – cheap and effective torn into pieces, especially as a final layer for painting on.

Blotting paper, brown wrapping paper, cartridge paper, sugar paper – coloured or plain, strong and particularly effective over large areas.

Gummed paper tape – quick and strong over small areas (see the sconce on page 106)

Tissue paper, paper napkins, crêpe paper – translucent and ideal for creasing into textured surfaces.

Handmade paper – your own (see page 34) or shop bought comes in a variety of weights and textures, has infinite uses and gives a distinguished finish to objects. *See also* Other Decorative Ingredients, page 12.

■ ADHESIVES

Non-toxic paste powder – safe for children.

Wallpaper paste – takes a while to dry, but easy to use when layering paper (see page 13); any type of gesso, traditional or acrylic, may be used on top of it (see Primers page 12).

Flour and water paste – inexpensive for layering paper, but may go lumpy and later grow mould.

PVA (polyvinyl acetate) wood glue/white glue – stronger for fastening paper to wood or metal and for joining cardboard pieces; in diluted form as a sealant to prevent cardboard, etc, from warping; and acrylic gesso is best used on top of it.

Rabbit-skin size – made from granules mixed with water, may be used instead of PVA/white glue if you want to paint an object with traditional gesso (see page 36).

Epoxy resin – can be used as a substitute for varnish or for very strong joins, but not for use by children and not easy for layering paper.

Vegetable glue – most suitable for adding material to finished objects, e.g. lining a box with fabric.

■ TAPES

Masking tape – fixes plastic wrap/saran wrap round a mould and secures glued joins until they are dry, when it is best replaced by gummed paper tape, though some makers do not bother.

Gummed paper tape – strengthens glued joins and is occasionally used instead of layers of pasted paper pieces (see page 106).

Gummed plastic parcel tape – useful for securing joins of large wooden moulds.

■ PASTE BOWL

Virtually any kind of mixing bowl – plastic, glass or porcelain – is suitable for mixing wallpaper paste or holding diluted PVA/white glue, etc. In a container with an airtight lid or sealed with plastic wrap/saran wrap, paste will last for several days.

■ MOULDS AND FRAMEWORKS

Many household objects (see following page) make suitable moulds for layering paper upon (see page 13), but bear in mind that, if the object narrows at any point, you may have to cut the papier mâché in half with a scalpel to remove it:

Balloons – of any shape or size are good for layering paper upon (see page 17).

Smooth-sided cardboard with corrugated interior, corrugated cardboard, flexible cardboard, rigid or flexible sheets of card – useful as basis for boxes, puppet theatre, mirror or picture frames, brooches, bracelets, etc; re-use old packaging whenever possible.

Modelling clay/plastic (plasticine) – used for shaping into objects to cast in a plaster mould (see page 27) or for creating details with/without layered paper on top.

Bowl of
wallpaper paste

Pencil and felt pen

White emulsion paint (primer)

Artists' brushes   Household paint brush

Petroleum jelly (releasing agent)

Masking tape

Balloons (for moulds)

Metal ruler/cutting edge

Cardboard, pink and
white newspapers,
cartridge or sugar paper

Scalpel

Modelling plastic

Scissors

Craft knife with
retractable blade

Wrapping paper, tissue paper, foil and photocopy (decoration)

Gouache paints (decoration)

Polyurethane varnish (sealer)

PVA/white glue

Plastic wrap/saran wrap (releasing agent)

Chickenwire – for creating an armature with pulp or layered paper on top (see page 30) and with a wooden substructure for larger pieces, e.g. lamp on page 90.

Wood – provides a strong framework for chickenwire armatures, for shelves, cupboards, etc, and for creating large frames to hold plaster/gypsum for moulds.

Plaster of Paris/gypsum – for creating moulds (see page 27).

■ RELEASING AGENTS

These prevent pulp or pasted paper from adhering to a mould:

Plastic wrap/saran wrap – comes in a roll, is secured in place with masking tape, and is used on simple shapes such as bowls, trays, woks, etc.

Petroleum jelly – most useful on intricate moulds or when you do not mind being left with a greasy surface to the papier mâché. Always remove any excess, otherwise it will cause difficulty later when you come to paint and decorate.

Soft soap or washing-up liquid – alternative to petroleum jelly.

■ FILLERS

Used to add bulk to paper pulp (see page 25):

Ground chalk/whiting – available from chemists and craft shops, it is the most commonly used filler.

Fine sawdust – may be used half and half with ground chalk/whiting, or as a cheap substitute for it.

■ CUTTERS

All of the following will be useful at one time or another:

Scissors, scalpel and a craft knife with a retractable blade – useful for a variety of purposes; special paper scissors are advisable.

Wire-cutters/tin-snips – for cutting wire and chickenwire.

Pair of pliers – for shaping chickenwire and wire.

Saws – a handsaw for lengths or planks of wood, and a jigsaw for cutting out intricate shapes.

Liquidizer/blender – for making pulp (see page 25).

■ MARKERS

A soft pencil and/or a fine felt-tip pen are needed for marking cutting lines and for outlining decorative designs on white emulsion or other sealant primers before painting.

◀ **Some basic equipment**

◀ **A selection of moulds
on which to layer paper**

At this point some people prefer to let the work dry between the application of each subsequent layer, but there is no vital necessity to do so; it simply means the object will dry more quickly.

Add the next and subsequent layers in alternate directions. If the object you are making is going to have a lid, check that the lid will still fit before adding further layers.

After six layers done in one sitting, it is advisable to let the object dry over a couple of days before proceeding.

The number of layers you choose to apply depends not only on how thick you want the finished object to be and the thickness of the paper being used but also on whether you intend strengthening it with a priming coat of gesso (see page 36) and/or a hard varnish sealant (see page 12). Experimentation is part of the fun!

Papier mâché is least likely to buckle when left to dry naturally on a cake rack in a warm room or in an airing cupboard for two or three days; some makers, however, 'bake' their work in a conventional oven or a microwave (no metallic moulds) in a low to medium setting until dry. Again timing is a matter of experience.

When you have as many layers as you require and the object has dried out, remove it from the mould by twisting it gently. If it gets stuck, try to ease round the edge with a palette knife; if that does not work, you may have to cut the paper with a craft knife or scalpel and then repair the damage with PVA/white glue and more papier mâché. If you wish to add a rim, spout, handle, base, etc, this is the stage at which to do so (see pages 18–25).

If you want to give the object a hard surface and prevent warping or paint from spreading, you can seal it with a thin coat of PVA/white glue or a layer of acrylic or traditional gesso (see page 36).

When the vessel is dry, coat it with emulsion paint. When this primer is dry, the object is ready to decorate.

When the decorated object is completely dry, apply a coat of sealer such as matt or gloss varnish (see page 12).

◄ **Decorating with pieces of wrapping paper**

■ LAYERING PAPER OVER A BALLOON

Balloons make versatile moulds because they come in many shapes and sizes. Long ones can, for instance, be used for creating cylindrical vases or cut into sections for bracelets, while with round ones you can make bowls, jugs or vases large and small. There is a chance that the balloon may burst once it is covered in papier mâché so take protective measures!

EQUIPMENT AND MATERIALS

Plastic sheeting or plastic
  bags
Bowl of wallpaper paste
Balloon

Newspaper and/or wall-
  lining paper
Cup/small bowl (as stand
  for drying)
Scissors or craft knife

METHOD Cover your work surface with plastic so that the sticky balloon will not adhere to it or, if you prefer to work with the balloon on your lap, then cover that with an old plastic carrier bag.

Mix the wallpaper paste in a bowl following the maker's instructions.

Blow up the balloon and tie a knot in the neck.

Rip the paper into strips or squares of appropriate size. Dip each piece in the paste, remove the excess with your fingers and smooth it on to the balloon, over-lapping each piece slightly.

If you are making a bowl, start from the bottom of the balloon and work upwards, stopping when you have reached the desired height.

If you are making a vase or a jug, you can start papering from the top downwards.

Once the first layer is completed, you can either set this aside to dry before continuing or you can proceed to add further layers. But, if the paper layers start to slip around out of position, stop. Remove any excess paste and paper until the layers are stable, and then let it all dry out thoroughly before resuming work.

Altogether you will need to cover the desired area with about eight layers of paper to create a substantial object.

If you want to make a flat-bottomed bowl, bravely puncture the balloon when the paper is almost dry but still damp, and slap the bottom of the bowl on a flat surface. Alternative methods are given on page 21.

For anything else, however, wait until the papier mâché is thoroughly dry before removing the balloon by unting the knot or bursting it with a pin. Trim the rim with scissors, if appropriate.

If you are making a bowl, see pages 21 and 18 for instructions on how to create a base and appropriate rim.

▲ Applying the third layer on a balloon

▲ Trimming a rim with scissors

If you are making a vase, for the top opening either cut a hole in the paper with scissors or gently rip the paper open with your fingers and remove the balloon. Then follow the directions on pages 21 and 20 for making a base and neck.

Once any additional features have been added (base, rim, etc), the dried papier mâché is ready for sealing, if you so wish, with PVA/white glue or with layers of gesso (see page 36), an optional primer coat of white emulsion paint, decorating and finally sealing with varnish (see page 12).

▲ Moulding pulp for earrings

▲ Attaching 'fish hooks'

▲ Brushing on a coat of gesso before decorating

■ HOW TO MAKE EARRINGS

EQUIPMENT AND MATERIALS

Scallop shell or mould	**Craft knife/scalpel**
Modelling clay	**Acrylic gesso or materials**
Plaster of Paris/gypsum	**and equipment for**
Mixing bowl	**making traditional gesso**
Materials and equipment	**(see page 36)**
for making paper pulp	**Brushes**
(see page 25)	**Gouache paints, etc, to**
Petroleum jelly	**decorate**
PVA/white glue	**Varnish**
Fastenings ('fish	
hooks'/clips, etc)	

METHOD The simplest method is to shape pulp directly into a scallop shell mould (see below). Alternatively you can impress part of a small scallop shell into modelling clay and make one or more moulds using plaster of Paris/gypsum (see page 27). A third alternative is to cut cardboard to the same scallop shape and then, with your fingers or a small palette knife, form the pulp on top of the card; but this is a more time-consuming method, especially if you wish to make several pairs of earrings.

To make finely textured pulp, shred good quality paper, e.g. typing paper. Soak it, boil it, liquidize it and then push it through a fine sieve. Squeeze most of the water out of the paper before stirring in ready-mixed wallpaper paste and linseed oil. (Quantities will vary, but, as a rough guide, add two tablespoons of linseed oil to a small washing-up bowl of mashed paper and paste.) Mix thoroughly. Add filler as necessary until the pulp is mouldable – dryish but sticky.

Cover the scallop mould with petroleum jelly, remove any excess and then press the pulp into the mould(s). Leave to dry.

To make round beads roll small quantities of pulp between the palms of your hands until they are evenly shaped. Leave to dry.

To insert 'fish hooks' for pierced ears and tiny metal loops for suspending beads, etc., delicately make an appropriate sized hole with a craft knife or scalpel in the scallop or bead and fix the metal attachments in place with PVA/white glue.

Using a brush, cover the scallops, beads, etc, with three thin layers of gesso (see page 36), allowing for each layer to dry before applying the next. For decorating ideas see pages 75–81 and opposite.

▶ **The finished earrings (Julie Howells)**

PROJECTS

·VESSELS·

CAROLINE GIBBS

Metallic bowls and dishes

EQUIPMENT AND MATERIALS

Bowls, dishes, etc, as moulds	Brushes
Rabbit-skin glue granules	Equipment and materials for making gesso (see page 36)
Mixing bowl	Fine sandpaper/glasspaper
Water	Bole (powdered clay), various colours
Double saucepan or large saucepan with heat-resistant bowl inside	Transfer metal leaf – silver, gold, etc
Plastic wrap/saran wrap or petroleum jelly	Goldsize (oil-based varnish)
Masking tape	Fine wire wool (optional)
Newspapers	

METHOD Make a fairly strong mix of rabbit-skin glue granules and water in a bowl and leave it to soak overnight. Next day heat a double saucepan of water near to boiling point and pour the size into the inner pan; keep it warm, but do not let the size boil.

Cover the outside of a large bowl or dish with petroleum jelly or with plastic wrap/saran wrap secured by masking tape, and stand it upside down. Tear some newspapers into pieces about 2.5cm (1in) square and dampen them with water (no glue) before applying the first layer to the mould.

To build up the second, third and fourth layers of paper apply the warm rabbit-skin size with a brush to each piece of paper in order to glue it in place. Add further layers if you wish.

When the layers of paper are dry, remove the object from the mould. Make a quantity of traditional gesso (see page 36), checking that there are no air bubbles in it. (Do not use acrylic gesso as this may flake.) With a brush apply six or more thin layers of gesso inside and out. (The water in the gesso will penetrate the paper bowl and distort it to give a crinkled, battered look.)

When dry, carefully smooth the surface of the final layer with fine sandpaper/glasspaper, paying particular attention to the rim, where extra gesso will have gathered because the bowl is upside down.

Paint on three thin coats of bole in the shade of your choice, allowing each layer to dry before applying the next. This provides a good base on which to gild.

Then gild the object with one or more layers of leaf in the colour of your choice. Double gild to achieve opacity, and burnish the leaf with wire wool if you want it to shine. Remember, too, that an attractive finish is created by oxidizing silver leaf. (If you are interested in this rather specialist art, why not read an authoritative book on gilding or take a course in water gilding?)

Finally protect the object with a coat of varnish.

Bowls with a textured surface

EQUIPMENT AND MATERIALS

100g (4oz) coloured paper (not newspaper or magazines)

Saucepan

Water

Liquidizer/blender

25g (1oz) PVA/white glue

Bowl for mixing

Bowl(s) as mould(s)

Plastic wrap/saran wrap

Masking tape

Fragments of material (optional) – silk, foil, muslin, etc

Disposable cellulose cleaning cloths

Newspapers

Metallic acrylic paints/ordinary acrylic paints/coloured metallic powder paints/non-tarnishing wax gilt (as for picture frames)/metallic oil pastels/gold leaf and water-based gold size, etc

Brushes

Matt varnish

METHOD Tear the paper into small pieces, soak it for a while in warm water and then boil it, before blending it into a fairly fine pulp. Pour the pulp into a bowl and drain off the surface water. Mix in the PVA/white glue.

Line the inside of the mould with plastic wrap/saran wrap secured in position with masking tape. Press dampened fragments of fabric, if desired, randomly round the interior. Then firmly press handfuls of pulp on top of the fragments and around the inside of the mould. To dry the pulp and compact it effectively roll a cleaning cloth into a ball and press it firmly against the pulp. Repeat this process until the pulp is dryish and stable.

Round the rim pinch the pulp between forefinger and thumb if you wish to create a frilly edge.

If you wish to make several small bowls from a single mould, the damp pulp bowl can be removed from the mould by holding the plastic wrap/saran wrap and gently lifting it out. Carefully remove the wrap and leave the pulp bowl on top of a thick layer of newspapers to dry for several days in a warm place.

Once thoroughly dry, use the paints, etc, suggested above to decorate the bowl, highlighting the texture of the pulp to create an antique look. Seal the bowl with matt varnish.

CAROL HILL

Footed fish bowls and vases

EQUIPMENT AND MATERIALS

Bowls as moulds – I large, I small	PVA/white glue
	White emulsion paint
Balloons as moulds	Brushes
Petroleum jelly	Materials and equipment
Newspapers, etc	for making gesso (see
Bowl of wallpaper paste	page 36)
Craft knife	Gouache or acrylic paints
Cardboard	Semi-gloss water-based
Masking tape	varnish

METHOD Bowls first. Cover the insides of both bowls with petroleum jelly. Over the inside of the larger bowl mould pasted paper strips (see page 13) – Louise Pearson builds up at least eight layers in one sitting, leaving the paper to stand proud of the rim by about 2.5cm (1in). While the paper is still damp and malleable, roll it over to form the basis of the rounded lip.

Once that is dry, paste thinner, smaller strips over the rim until you achieve the desired thickness.

Cover the inside of the smaller bowl with eight layers of pasted paper pieces and, when dry, trim the rim neatly with scissors or a craft knife (see page 18). Then, following the method on page 19, add a flat cardboard rim. Leave to dry.

Glue the bottom of the small bowl to the bottom of the big bowl, and fill the join with small rolls of pasted paper. The raised decorative motifs are cut from cardboard, pasted in place and then built up by pasting five layers of paper pieces over them. Once all is dry, paint the footed bowl with white emulsion, repair any cracks or holes with gesso, emulsion over those repairs and then decorate with gouache or acrylic paints. Seal with three coats of water-based varnish, allowing each coat to dry before applying the next.

Now for the vase. Following the methods described on page 17, mould eight layers of pasted paper pieces on to a large balloon right up to the neck. The flat base

is made by cutting a hole in the bottom of the dried paper balloon and filling this with a circle of cardboard, as described on page 21, method 4. Make a series of vertical cuts round the neck of the vase and splay out the paper, dampening it slightly first, if necessary. Paste small paper strips first horizontally round and then vertically over the rim until the desired shape is achieved. As decorative features thin paper rolls are stuck on in twirly shapes with PVA/white glue and masking tape. Then emulsion, repair, decorate and seal in the same manner as the footed bowl.

Boxes

EQUIPMENT AND MATERIALS

Planks of wood	Waterproof acrylic black
Handsaw	ink
Hammer and nails	Brushes
Tissue paper	Watercolour paints
Bowl of wallpaper paste	Matt cellulose lacquer
Pair of metal hinges and	spray
pins	

METHOD Make a wooden box, but do not yet attach the lid. Cover it inside and out – the lid as well – with as many layers as you like of pasted tissue paper pieces until the wood is invisible. To add texture wrinkle the paper or, as Nicola Sargent has done on one of her boxes, paste on snaking rolls of paper to the top of the lid and sides.

Affix the metal hinges to the box and lid, then decorate with ink and watercolours before applying several layers of protective sealant.

Blue bowl

EQUIPMENT AND MATERIALS

Large bowl as mould

Plastic wrap/saran wrap

Masking tape

Newspapers, etc

Bowl of wallpaper paste

Materials and equipment
  for making gesso (see
  page 36)

Brushes

Fine sandpaper/glasspaper

Incising tool

Blue bole (powdered clay)

Blue oil paint

Gold transfer leaf

Fine wire wool

Matt cellulose lacquer
  spray

METHOD Using the method described on page 13, mould ten layers of pasted paper pieces on the inside of a large bowl. When the paper is dry, apply twenty thin layers of gesso, sanding each dry layer smooth before applying the next.

With an incising tool, inscribe the pattern of your choice in the gesso.

Paint the whole bowl with two coats of bole and sand them off patchily when dry. Emphasize the incised pattern with blue oil paint. Once this is dry, apply one or more layers of gold leaf, as desired. When dry, burnish the leaf with thin wire wool before sealing with varnish.

VESSELS

47

Tubular pot

EQUIPMENT AND MATERIALS

Flexible smooth cardboard
  or card
Scissors
Masking tape
Newspapers, etc
Bowl of wallpaper paste
Materials and equipment
  for making gesso (see
  page 36)

Brushes
Waterproof Indian ink
Gouache paints
Semi-gloss cellulose
  lacquer spray

METHOD Cut a length of cardboard or card and roll it into a tube. Tape it firmly in shape. Cut a circle of cardboard or card to fit snugly inside one end of the tube and tape it in place.

Cover the pot inside and out with at least five layers of pasted paper pieces, taking care to make the rim as smooth as possible.

Once the paper pot is dry, four layers of gesso are applied. Allow time for each coat to dry before applying the next – it does not take long.

Nicola Sargent then draws on the outline of her pattern in waterproof ink and fills it in with gouache colours, before finally covering the pot with several layers of protective lacquer.

For fresh flowers, insert a glass or plastic container inside the pot to protect papier mâché from water

NICOLA SARGENT

Hanging pot

EQUIPMENT AND MATERIALS

Balloon as mould	Brushes
Newspapers, etc	Incising tool
Bowl of wallpaper paste	Silver transfer leaf
Scissors and craft knife	Acrylic waterproof black
Materials and equipment	ink
for making gesso (see	Semi gloss lacquer spray
page 36)	Chains and hooks

METHOD Following the method described on page 17, mould a vase shape on a balloon with at least five layers of pasted paper pieces. Open the neck by making vertical scissor cuts all round. Fan open the paper and strengthen the neck with further horizontal and vertical pasted paper strips until you achieve the shape desired. Leave it to dry.

Using scissors or a craft knife, make three holes near the rim of the pot and tidy the rough edges with paste.

Apply six thin layers of gesso, following the method described on page 36. When the final layer is dry, delicately inscribe a pattern into the gesso with an incising tool. Remove any dust clinging to the vessel and float on one or more layers of silver leaf. After a while, left like this, the leaf will tarnish to the shade of Nicola Sargent's pot.

Acrylic ink is applied to the incised pattern and then the pot is given a protective coat of lacquer. Thread the hooks through the holes round the rim and attach the chains for hanging.

NICOLA SARGENT

Muslin bowls with beads

EQUIPMENT AND MATERIALS

Square and round bowls
  as moulds

Plastic wrap/saran wrap

Masking tape

Muslin or fine cheesecloth

Bowl of wallpaper paste

Newspapers, etc

Scissors or scalpel

White emulsion paint

Brushes

Gloss yacht varnish

For square bowl:

Acrylic and gold paints

Glass 'gemstones' with flat
  backs

PVA/white glue

For gold bowl:

Gold, black and purple
  acrylic paints

Coarse needle and black
  silk string

16 black and 8 white
  wooden beads

8 plastic mirror 'scimitars'

For striped bowl:

Orange and peacock blue
  acrylic paints

Coarse needle and black
  silk string

8 matt black, 8 faceted
  'jet' and 8 natural wood
  beads

METHOD All three bowls are created using the same basic methods. Cover the inside of the mould with plastic wrap/saran wrap secured by masking tape. Dip a piece of muslin in the wallpaper paste and line the mould with it. Apply four or more layers of pasted paper pieces and, for the two round bowls, apply a final layer of pasted muslin. In the case of the square bowl, let the layers protrude above the rim of the mould to form rough points.

With scissors or a scalpel, trim the rims of the round bowls neatly (see page 18). Trim the rim of the square bowl into spikes if necessary. Coat all three bowls with white emulsion and leave to dry.

Decorate the square bowl in shades of orange, peacock and gold, outline the rim in black and, when dry, affix the glass stones to the inside with PVA/white glue. Apply a coat of yacht varnish.

For the gold bowl, paint on a layer of gold paint and patterns in black and purple. Make eight small holes round the rim with a scalpel. Coat it with yacht varnish. Using eight lengths of silk string, tie a knot in one end of each, thread on two black beads, one white one and a 'scimitar'. Thread a needle with the string through into the inside of the bowl, round the lip and back to the outside, where the loose end is neatly knotted.

The striped bowl is painted orange and blue, and again eight holes are made round the rim. Apply a coat of yacht varnish. Each of the pieces of silk string is knotted at one end, has three beads put on it and the loose end knotted inside the bowl.

Golden boxes

EQUIPMENT AND MATERIALS

Mounting board or any
  good card
PVA/white glue
Typing paper/newspaper/
  brown wrapping paper (if
  handmade paper is thin)
Materials and equipment
  for making paper (see
  page 34) or shop-bought
  handmade paper

Bowl of wallpaper paste
Water repellant sealer
Brush
Spirit-based paper varnish
  or semi-gloss household
  interior varnish

METHOD Maureen Hamilton-Hill uses techniques similar to those described on page 28, but, instead of cardboard, she prefers to use mounting card and attaches the pieces of the box with adhesive only – no tape as it is too coarse for her work.

To achieve a speckled look, she applies acrylic paints or fabric dyes to plain paper before making pulp for her handmade paper.

If the handmade paper is thin, apply a pasted layer of typing paper, newspaper or brown wrapping paper first, taking particular care over the corners.

Finally the box should be given a waterproof coating and, when that is dry, a coat of matt or semi-gloss varnish.

For a paperweight, cover large pebbles from the beach with a layer of pasted handmade paper sealed with varnish

MAUREEN HAMILTON-HILL

VESSELS

Vase and jug with pleated necks, and seahorse vase

EQUIPMENT AND MATERIALS

For vase and jug:

Handmade or good quality
  paper

Bowl of wallpaper paste

Plastic or paper bag (as
  mould)

For seahorse vase:

Materials and equipment
  for making pulp (see
  p.25)

Cold-water material dye

Balloon

Box of coarse sand
  (optional)

PVA/white glue

Gold and metallic paints

Matt varnish

Brush

METHOD The vase and jug with pleated necks are both made from Miriam Troth's own handmade paper, which is fairly thick. For the main body of both, large pieces of pasted paper were moulded round a malleable, air-filled bag. A strip of paper folded into pleats was pasted to the necks of both vessels and, in the case of the jug, simply extended downwards while damp to form a handle.

The conical body of the seahorse vase began as dyed pulp moulded on to part of a balloon, with extra pulp added to form the pointed end. The seahorses and starfish, which are rounded on both sides, are shaped by hand – Miriam Troth uses a box of sand to hold them while they dry, but they could be made in two halves and glued together (see page 27).

After lengthy drying, the pieces are secured to the main vessel with PVA/white glue. Metallic paints are then smeared on the dyed pulp with fingers or a brush.

Finally all three vessels are sealed with a matt varnish.

MIRIAM TROTH

Giant dish and Ali Baba jar

EQUIPMENT AND MATERIALS

Pair of protective gloves

Coarse-gauge chickenwire

Wire-cutters/tin-snips

Pair of pliers

Newspapers

Bowl of wallpaper paste

Pliable cardboard

PVA/white glue

Masking tape

Scissors

Sand (optional)

Wall-lining paper

White emulsion paint

Acrylic paints, wax
   crayons, waterproof
   black ink

Brushes

Matt paper varnish

METHOD The huge dish is formed from a large circle of chickenwire with the rim turned in and the spiky ends tucked away using a pair of pliers. Bend the wire into a concave shape and cover both sides with six or more layers of pasted pieces of newspaper. As a final layer apply large pasted pieces of wall-lining paper to create a smooth painting surface.

Coat the dish with emulsion and, when dry, decorate in acrylics and crayons, outling the pattern in water-proof ink. Finally apply a coat of paper varnish to prevent discolouration.

The basis of the jar is also chickenwire. Its round main body is comprised of two pieces, each carefully cut to the shape of Mercator's flat projection of the Earth as shown in an atlas, i.e. virtually straight at top and bottom, but strongly curved on either side. Using the spiky raw edges, these two pieces are carefully joined together. A circle of chicken wire forms a base.

Before attaching a circle of chickenwire for the neck, cover the inside of the jar with at least five layers of pasted newspaper and a final layer of wall-lining paper. To weight the base and stabilize the jar, put a fair quantity of sand between one or more of the layers covering the inside of the base.

Attach the wire neck and cover it with three layers of pasted newspaper pieces. To create a rounded lip, attach a roll of newspaper to the outer rim, secure it in place with masking tape and cover it with at least two layers of paper. When the whole jar is covered in at least five layers of newspaper pieces and is dry, attach two cardboard handles with PVA/white glue and masking tape. Cover the rest of the jar and handles with a layer of pasted wall-lining paper. Coat the jar with emulsion and then decorate as before. Seal with a coat of matt paper varnish.

MALCOLM TEMPLE

Vessels with stalks, leaves and letters

EQUIPMENT AND MATERIALS

Bowls and a dish as
  moulds

Plastic wrap/saran wrap

Masking tape

Handmade paper (see
  page 34) or top quality
  coloured paper

Bowl of wallpaper paste

Dried plant stalks and
  leaves

Photocopies of letters or
  letters cut from news-
  papers

Waterproofer

Spirit-based paper varnish

Brushes

METHOD For translucent vessels Maureen Hamilton-
Hill generally uses her own thin handmade paper,
which is made solely from pulp and water (see page
34). However, she also sometimes uses coloured paper
napkins, pieces of fabric – yellow silk is a favourite –
and dried or pressed plant material.

Cover the inside of the mould in plastic wrap/saran
wrap affixed with masking tape. Tear handmade paper
(several different colours, if you wish) into pieces and
dampen it. Paste the pieces and build up three or four
layers for smallish vessels, up to six layers for larger vessels. With thin layers the finish is smoother and joins
less noticeable – unless, of course, the joins are part of
the design.

The bowl on the left features pressed plant stalks
inserted between the second and third layers, while for
the right-hand bowl pressed leaves were pasted on to
the final layer of paper when it was still damp. The dish
in the front has photocopied letters pasted on to the top
layer and partly over-painted in diluted white emulsion.

Once the vessels are dry, apply a coat of waterproofer
and, when that too is dry, seal pale paper objects with
paper varnish so that they do not discolour; darker
objects may be sealed with household interior quality
varnish.

MAUREEN HAMILTON-HILL

Jug with scene inset

EQUIPMENT AND MATERIALS

Large jug as mould	Fine sandpaper/glasspaper
Newspapers	Poster paints or similar
Bowl of wallpaper paste	Matt varnish
Scalpel	Coarse sewing needle
PVA/white glue	Embroidery cotton
Small bowl as mould	*For scene furnishings:*
Pencil	Fine wire
Masking tape	Balsa wood or similar
Gummed paper tape	softwood
String	Tiny found objects or
White emulsion paint	doll's house articles
Brushes	Craft knife

METHOD If you wish, the jug can be moulded on a balloon (see page 17) and then a rim, handle and base may be added (see pages 18, 23 and 20), but Melanie Williams uses a large porcelain jug as a mould. Over the outside, including the handle, a layer of damp, unpasted newspaper pieces is applied instead of a sealer, followed by five or more layers of pasted paper pieces.

When these are dry, carefully slice the paper jug in half vertically – through the handle and avoiding where the scene will be inset.

Glue the two pieces together immediately, before they have time to warp, with PVA/white glue. Secure the join with strips of masking tape. When the glue is dry, carefully remove the masking tape and replace it with gummed paper tape for strength.

Enlarge the spout and rim, if you so wish, with further layers of pasted pieces of newspaper. Neaten the rim by pasting strips of paper over the edge from inside to outside (see page 18) and leave to dry.

Meanwhile, on the inside of a small bowl, build up five or more layers of newspaper pieces, the first layer unpasted so that it will not adhere to the mould. When dry, remove the paper bowl from the mould, hold it against the outside of the paper jug and mark in pencil the outline of the bowl's rim on the jug. With a scalpel cut out a hole and affix the paper bowl in place with PVA/white glue and masking tape. When dry, replace the latter with gummed paper tape. Secure the join with small strips of pasted paper and leave to dry.

Smooth any rough patches with sandpaper/glasspaper before brushing the whole jug with a coat of white emulsion. With a pencil outline your chosen decorative features. The raised letters are formed by pieces of string affixed with glue or paste and then emulsioned. Paint the jug, including the 'walls' and chequered 'floor' of the inset scene.

Melanie's birdcage is fashioned from fine wire, the cupboard shaped with a craft knife from balsa wood, and the vase of flowers from tiny pieces of pasted paper.

The jug is sprayed with matt varnish. Once dry, the rims are blanket stitched, strengthening the structure and providing an original decorative feature.

Attractive raised patterns can be created
by gluing on string of various sizes and textures

Casket

EQUIPMENT AND MATERIALS

Sheets of smooth-sided corrugated cardboard	Bowl of wallpaper paste
Metal ruler	Modelling plastic
Pencil or felt-tip pen	Petroleum jelly
Craft knife and scissors	White emulsion paint
PVA/white glue	Gouache paints
Masking tape	Waterproof black ink
Gummed paper tape	Brushes
Newspapers	Gloss polyurethane
Bowl of wallpaper paste	varnish

METHOD Beginning with the base, cut from the cardboard a rectangle 30.5cm × 23cm (12in × 9in), two strips 30.5cm × 6.5cm (12in × 2½in), and two strips 23cm × 6.5cm (9in × 2½in). On one side of each strip cut out simple curves or whatever shape you prefer. Seal both sides of all the pieces with diluted PVA/white glue, and allow it to dry before assembling them.

Apply PVA/white glue to the edges of the large rectangle and to the appropriate edges of the four strips. To keep the pieces in place until the glue dries apply strips of masking tape to each join before gluing the next one. When dry, replace the masking tape with gummed paper tape to strengthen the joins.

For the body of the casket cut two cardboard rectangles 28cm × 12.5cm (11in × 5in), and two 20.5cm × 12.5cm (8in × 5in). Seal all the pieces with a coating of diluted PVA/white glue. When dry, join these four pieces to each other and affix them centrally on top of the base with PVA/white glue and masking tape, replacing the latter by gummed paper tape once the glue is dry.

To create the lid begin by cutting one rectangle of cardboard 29cm × 21.5cm (11½in × 8½in), and two pieces 27.5cm × 20cm (10¾in × 7¾in). Seal all three pieces with diluted PVA/white glue and, when dry, glue the two smaller pieces together, one flat on top of the other (see page 00 on making a box).

Next glue both of these pieces to the centre of the large rectangle. Keep them all in place with masking tape until the glue is completely dry; then replace with gummed paper tape.

For the 'roof' on the lid cut two equilateral triangles of 18cm (7in) and two rectangles 25cm × 5cm (9¾in × 2in). Seal all four pieces with a coat of diluted PVA/white glue and join them together in the manner described above. Then glue and tape the roof centrally on top of the lid.

For the ridge cut a piece of cardboard 25cm × 5cm (9¾in × 2in) and cut a serpentine pattern along one side. Attach the plain side to the ridge with glue and tape as before.

Three layers of pasted paper pieces are then applied over the whole casket, inside and out. Leave to dry for at least two days.

Meanwhile, shape modelling plastic into eighteen balls plus one egg shape and coat them with petroleum jelly. Cover them with five layers of small pasted paper pieces and allow to dry for several days. Then cut them in half, remove the modelling plastic and glue the hemispheres round the base of the box and along the ridge, securing them with masking tape while the glue dries. Remove the masking tape and apply a layer of tiny pasted paper pieces to the joins.

When all is dry, coat the casket inside and out with two layers of white emulsion, allowing time for each to dry.

Draw on your design in pencil and fill in the background colours. Next do the overpainting and, once that is dry, use black ink to add outlines and details. Finally apply three coats of varnish, allowing plenty of drying time between each.

Fish pot with glasses

MATERIALS AND EQUIPMENT

Balloon as mould	**Masking tape**
Newspapers	**Modelling plastic**
Bowl of wallpaper paste	**White emulsion paint**
Cup or small bowl as	**Brushes**
stand for drying	**Poster, acrylic or gouache**
Cardboard	**paints**
Pencil	**PVA/white glue**
Craft knife	**Gloss varnish**

METHOD Blow up a balloon until it is pear-shaped and tie a knot in the neck. Then follow the directions on page 17 for layering pasted paper on a balloon. Once the paper layers are dry, burst the balloon and remove it. Cut a hole in what will be the top of the pot and neaten the rim with strips of pasted newspaper.

On a sheet of cardboard draw the two side fins and a tail of appropriate size, and cut them out with a craft knife. Cover all three pieces with at least two layers of pasted newspaper pieces and leave to dry.

From two circles of cardboard create a flat base for the pot, following the directions for method 2 on page 21.

Secure the tail to the open, slightly pointed, end of the paper balloon with masking tape, and cover the join inside and out with several layers of small pasted paper pieces. Affix the fins to either side of the pot with tape and pasted paper pieces.

The fish's features are moulded in modelling plastic straight on to the front of the pot. They are then covered in three or more layers of pasted paper pieces before being left to dry.

From cardboard cut out a simple pair of spectacles of a suitable size to fit behind the side fins. Bend the cardboard to form arms and then cover in two or more layers of pasted paper pieces.

Coat the pot and spectacles with emulsion and, when dry, decorate in the colours of your choice. Glue the spectacles in place. Lastly apply one or more coats of gloss varnish for strength and protection.

AMANDA GODDEN

·JEWELRY·

JULIE HOWELLS

Chestful of earrings and necklaces

EQUIPMENT AND MATERIALS

Modelling plastic or clay

Materials and equipment
  for making plaster
  moulds (see page 27)

Petroleum jelly

Materials and equipment
  for making pulp (see
  page 25) with typing
  paper

Sieve

Earring clips, 'fish-hooks',
  loops, etc

Coarse sewing needle

PVA/white glue

Acrylic gesso

Brushes

Gold paint or ink, acrylic
  paints, etc

Matt varnish

Tiny glass beads

Thread and clasp for
  necklace

METHOD For earrings, mould modelling plastic or clay into shell shapes or impress a tiny scallop shell into a small mound of plastic or clay (see page 27). Coat the mould with petroleum jelly and duplicate the shapes in a tray of plaster of Paris/gypsum (see page 27).

Make a suitable quantity of finely textured pulp from good quality typing paper (see page 25), which is pushed through a sieve before being mixed with the other ingredients. The pulp should be malleable – dryish, but sticky. Cover the plaster moulds with petroleum jelly and then press pulp firmly into them. Leave them to dry for several days.

To insert 'fish-hooks' for pierced ears and metal loops for suspending beads, etc, make holes through the dry pulp with a coarse sewing needle. Affix ear clips with PVA/white glue.

To make beads for necklaces or earrings, patiently mould pulp between the palms of your hands until perfectly round. Once dry, use a coarse needle to pierce a hole through each bead, if you want to thread them into a necklace.

Cover both earrings and beads in three coats of acrylic gesso, allowing each layer to dry before applying the next. (Julie Howells uses acrylic gesso because her pet rabbits, which have the run of her studio, enjoy eating traditional gesso, but will not touch acrylic.)

Apply a layer of gold ink or paint to earrings and beads before using a pointillist technique to paint layer upon layer of tiny coloured dots.

Finally seal the jewelry with a coat of matt varnish and attach miniature decorative beading, if you so wish, with PVA/white glue.

Earrings and brooches

EQUIPMENT AND MATERIALS

Secondhand earrings, *objets trouvés*, etc	Newspapers
	Bowl of wallpaper paste
Commercial fruit trays of moulded paper pulp	Metal earclips, 'fish-hooks', brooch pins, etc
Craft knife	Cardboard
Handmade or wrapping paper	Coarse sewing needle or scalpel
PVA/white glue	Fine sandpaper/glasspaper
Acrylic paints	Matt or semi-gloss varnish
Brushes	

METHOD Miriam Troth enjoys recycling materials and incorporating *objets trouvés* (often gleaned from car boot sales) in her own creations.

The oval earrings reminiscent of oyster shells are basically made from machine-moulded pulp trays with concave indentations used by fruiterers for transporting apples, etc. Miriam cuts out a pointed oval and covers it with handmade painted paper affixed with PVA/white glue. She then makes one or two slits lengthways through the concave shape. The areas outside the slits are bent upwards, away from the rest of the earring. The raw cut edges are delicately coloured.

Alternatively the pulp shape may be covered in several layers of small pasted paper pieces, painted in acrylics and then varnished.

Earring clips or 'fish-hooks', or even whole earrings, are then attached by tiny metal links inserted through the paper earrings via a hole made with a coarse sewing needle or scalpel.

Miriam's zig-zag brooches are made of dampened handmade paper pasted on to very damp cardboard, which is then pleated and left to dry before being cut into pieces with a sharp craft knife. A brooch pin is then attached to the back with PVA/white glue.

The rectangular and abstract brooches are of cardboard covered in several layers of paper pieces affixed with PVA/white glue. They are then sanded smooth and decorated in acrylic and metallic paints or are covered in handmade paper before being coated with varnish.

Bracelets, earrings and brooch

EQUIPMENT AND MATERIALS

Materials and equipment
  for making pulp (see
  page 25)

Crab claws

PVA/white glue

Brushes

White emulsion paint

Powder paints

Foil and cellophane sweet
  wrappers, etc

Scissors

Silver coins

Existing cheap earrings
  and brooches

Metal earring clips, brooch
  pins and links

Flat-backed glass 'jewels'

Matt and gloss varnish

METHOD The central bangle above is shaped freehand from paper pulp. While the pulp is damp, real crab claws are inset with PVA/white glue and extra pulp moulded round the bases. When dry, a coat of white emulsion is applied. Powder paints and foil are used to decorate the bangle.

The other bangle, on the left, is made in similar fashion, but with small silver coins inset into pulp instead of claws.

The fish earrings are modelled freehand from pulp. While the pulp is slightly damp, insert a metal 'fish-hook'. When dry, foil and cellophane wrappers are attached with PVA/white glue, with the cellophane twisted and trimmed with scissors into a tail.

The triple-tiered circular earrings are also made from pulp covered in sweet wrappers, but this time moulded on top of an ugly pair of existing earrings.

The 'jewelled' pendant earrings are again modelled freehand from pulp with glass jewels pressed into the damp pulp with a blob of glue. Metal links are also inserted at this stage. When dry, the pulp is painted a dull silver. Finally varnish is applied to the painted areas and metal ear-clips are glued to the backs.

The moon at the top of the brooch is shop bought with a pin already attached and is then covered in a thin layer of pulp. While the pulp is damp, a metal link from which to suspend the lower part of the brooch is inserted and the pulp left to dry. The lower part of the brooch is moulded freehand from pulp with any handy implement. Again the joining link is inserted through the damp pulp. Powder paints and metal foil are used to decorate before sealing with varnish.

Bangles and earrings

EQUIPMENT AND MATERIALS

Pliable cardboard or card

Scissors or a craft knife

Masking tape

Newspapers, etc

Bowl of wallpaper paste

Materials and equipment
for making pulp (see
page 25)

Fine sandpaper/glasspaper

White emulsion paint

Pencil or waterproof felt
pen

Acrylic paints

Waterproof black ink

Brushes

Gloss varnish

Metal loops and 'fish-
hooks' (for earrings)

METHOD To make a bangle, cut a strip of card or card-board approximately 5cm (2 inches) wide and roll it into a circle fixed in place with masking tape. Cover the card or cardboard with at least three layers of pasted paper pieces as smoothly as possible, especially on the inside. Leave to dry.

Make a small quantity of dryish paper pulp and apply this to the outside of the bangle to create a curved out-line. When the pulp has dried, go over the outside of the bangle with a piece of fine sandpaper/glasspaper to remove any irregularities.

Paint the bangle with white emulsion and leave to dry.

With a pencil or waterproof pen, draw a pattern on the outside and paint the strongly coloured areas. Use black waterproof ink or black acrylic paint to cover the inside of the bangle, the rims and the outlines. Finally apply two coats of gloss varnish.

The earrings are simply made from cardboard or card shapes, to which wire loops and fish-hooks have been attached before three or more layers of small pasted paper pieces are neatly applied. Once dry, they are dec-orated and sealed in the same way as the bangle.

Heart, fish and bird brooches

EQUIPMENT AND MATERIALS

Equipment and materials
  for making plaster
  moulds (see page 27)
Equipment and materials
  for making pulp (see
  page 25)
Petroleum jelly/releasing
  agent
Palette knife
White emulsion paint
Paint brushes
Gouache paints, various
  colours
Metallic brooch pins (from
  craft/art supplies shop)
PVA/white glue

METHOD Following the method described on page 27, make one or more plaster moulds of a heart, a fish or a bird. Then make a quantity of finely textured paper pulp, following the directions given in the recipe on page 25.

Cover the inside of the mould with petroleum jelly or other releasing agent. Press paper pulp firmly into the mould until it is full. Smooth the surface with a palette knife, removing any surplus pulp. Put the full mould in a warm, airy place to dry for several days.

When the paper is completely dry, paint the brooch with white emulsion paint. Decorate with one or two coats of gouache paints in the colours of your choice.

When the decoration is dry, apply a protective coat of varnish. Finally, affix a brooch pin to the back with PVA/white glue.

Using a plaster mould to produce several pieces at once allows more time for creative decoration

JEANETTE ORRELL

·INTERIORS·

Candlestick, mirror, pen/pencil holder, bottle coaster and napkin ring

EQUIPMENT AND MATERIALS

Corrugated and plain cardboard	Wrapping paper of fish or photocopies
Masking tape	Watercolour paints (optional)
Newspapers, etc	
PVA/white glue	Crackle varnish set
White emulsion paint	Matt varnish
Brushes	Fire retardant liquid
Gouache and gold paints	Small metal candle-holder
	Mirror

METHOD For the candlestick roll a length of cardboard, corrugated side out, into a tube and secure with masking tape. From smooth cardboard cut out a large star and with PVA/white glue affix it to one end of the tube as a base. Cut a smaller star for the top rim, cut a hole in it so that it will slip over the top of the tube and glue it in place.

Using PVA/white glue, paste on five layers of newspaper pieces both inside (as far as possible) and outside.

When dry, coat the candlestick with white emulsion, followed by a layer of pale green paint. The top and bottom edges are painted gold.

Using watercolours, colour in the fish on the wrapping paper or photocopies (the latter may need to be given a spray of fixative first). Cut out and glue on the fish. Next draw on and paint in some gold stars edged in waterproof ink.

To create a distressed appearance suggesting antiquity apply two layers of crackle varnish as per the maker's instructions. Once dry, apply a coat of matt varnish, plus a final coat of fire retardant inside and out. Lastly, insert the metal candle-holder in the top.

The pen/pencil holder, bottle coaster and napkin ring are made of smooth cardboard, using the same methods of construction and decoration as for the candlestick.

To make the mirror frame cut out a rectangle of thick, smooth cardboard, in the centre of which a rectangle is cut out slightly smaller than the piece of mirror. Around this central opening glue on flattened pasted rolls of newspaper to create a raised rim. Using PVA/white glue and masking tape, secure the mirror, face out, to the back of the cardboard.

Next cut a second rectangle of cardboard precisely the same size as the first and glue this on as a backing board to the mirror and cardboard front. Secure the edges with masking tape, if necessary. Then cover all the cardboard with at least four layers of pasted paper pieces.

Once dry, proceed to prime with emulsion, decorate and seal in the same manner as the candlestick. If any paint strays on to the mirror, this can be delicately scraped off with a scalpel.

Spice rack and stationery holder

EQUIPMENT AND MATERIALS

Cardboard	Newspapers, etc
Pencil or felt-tip pen	Bowl of wallpaper paste
Ruler	Ball of coarse string
Craft knife and scissors	White emulsion paint
PVA/white glue	Brushes
Masking tape	Gouache paints
Gummed paper tape	Matt varnish

METHOD For the two-shelf spice rack mark out on a sheet of cardboard with the aid of a pencil/pen and ruler the backing sheet, two matching end pieces, two matching shelf pieces and two identical front panels. With a craft knife cut out the backing piece and one each of the ends, the shelves and the fronts. Place the end, the shelf and the front piece on the outlines of their matching pairs, and check that the outlines and dimensions are the same. Cut out the second end, shelf and front pieces.

With PVA/white glue and masking tape secure the pieces together and leave to dry. Replace the masking tape with gummed paper tape for strength. Cover the whole rack with three layers of pasted paper pieces and set aside to dry. Then affix appropriate lengths of string to all external edges and joins with PVA/white glue and masking tape. When the glue is dry, cover the string and the rest of the rack with a layer of pasted paper pieces, taking care not to flatten the string too much while emphasizing its outline.

From cardboard cut out five hearts and cover them with a layer of pasted paper pieces, keeping the outline as crisp as possible. When they are dry, glue four to the front of the bottom shelf and one centre top.

Glue two curlicues of string to the upper part of the back panel and a further piece zig-zagging along the front of the top shelf. Cover all the string in a layer of pasted paper pieces and leave to dry.

Coat the rack with white emulsion before painting with watered gouaches and finally sealing with a matt varnish.

The stationery holder is made using the same techniques.

AMANDA BLUNDEN

Tulips in a blue jug

EQUIPMENT AND MATERIALS

For tulips:	For jug:
2 packets long, medium-gauge stub/florists' wire	Jug as a mould
Wire-cutters/tin-snips	Newspapers
Newspapers	Bowl of wallpaper paste
Bowl of flour and water paste or PVA/white glue	Scalpel
1 packet thick stub/florists' wire or poker wire	PVA/white glue
Fine sandpaper/glasspaper	Masking tape
White emulsion paint	Gummed paper tape
Brushes	Wire from old coathanger
Poster paints or similar	White emulsion paint
Matt varnish	Brushes
	Gold and blue paint
	Sponge
	Semi-gloss varnish

METHOD Each individual tulip petal is made separately by bending a length of stub/florists' wire to shape and twisting the two ends together at the base of the petal – do not trim the ends. With PVA/white glue or paste stick long thin strips of newspaper round and across the wire frame, keeping the edges smooth and adjusting the shape as you proceed. Cover each petal with three layers of paper and set aside to dry.

In one hand hold the wire ends of five petals round a length of thick wire, and with your other hand wind a pasted or glued strip of newspaper round all the wires. Begin just below the base of the petals and spiral the paper gradually down the stem. Add further layers, but set aside to dry before the newspaper becomes too mushy. Add further layers until the wire stem is covered. Leave to dry and then, if necessary, smooth the surfaces with fine sandpaper/glasspaper.

Cover the whole flower and stalk with a coat of white emulsion. When that is dry, paint the petals and stalks in the shades of your choice and finally seal them with a coat of matt varnish.

Although jugs are usually based on layers of pasted newspaper pieces moulded on a balloon (see page 17), Melanie Williams often prefers to mould layers on an existing jug of attractive proportions. The outside of the jug and handle ends are covered in a layer of damp, unpasted newspaper pieces. Remember to leave paper protruding above the rim. Five or more layers of pasted paper pieces are then applied and left to dry.

Using a scalpel, delicately cut the paper jug vertically in half and remove it from the mould. Immediately stick the two halves together again with PVA/white glue, and secure in place with masking tape. When the join has dried, replace the masking tape with pieces of gummed paper tape for strength. Cover the joins with a layer of pasted paper pieces.

To smooth the rim, moisten the paper round it with paste and bend it over neatly. If necessary, apply one or more layers of pasted paper strips over the rim from inside to outside (see page 18).

Handles can be made in several ways (see page 23), but Melanie sometimes chooses to change the position and shape of the original handle, so she has her own method. She dampens the rough paper round the existing handle holes with wallpaper paste and folds it together to cover the gaps. If necessary, she adds fresh pasted paper pieces inside and out to create a smooth surface. The basis of the new handle is coathanger wire pushed into the jug through two small holes made with a scalpel. The wire ends are bent flat against the inside of the jug, secured with masking tape and pasted over with pieces of paper. The wire handle is then bound in layer upon layer of long pasted strips of paper and left to dry.

Following a coat of white emulsion paint, a layer of gold paint is applied. When that is dry, rich blue paint is sponged on. For protection the whole jug is given one or more coats of semi-gloss varnish.

These tulips in a jug were inspired by a Cézanne painting – why not try Van Gogh's sunflowers, for instance

Firescreen

EQUIPMENT AND MATERIALS

Sheet of rigid board, e.g. medium-density fibre-board (MDF)

Pencil or felt-tip pen

Newspapers

Bowl of wallpaper paste

White emulsion paint

Brushes

Gouache paints

Wrapping paper or wallpaper

Oil glaze

Semi-gloss varnish

Jigsaw

Fine sandpaper/glasspaper

Metal hinges and pins

Hammer

METHOD On a sheet of rigid board sketch with a pencil or felt pen the outline of a firescreen to suit the dimensions of your fireplace.

Cover the area of the screen with a layer of pasted pieces of newspaper. Over the lower part which is going to look like a marble urn or vase apply a coat of white emulsion. When that is dry, paint on a stone-coloured background in gouache and add *trompe l'oeil* marble streaks. (Alternatively you could paste shop-bought marbled paper over this area instead.)

From floral wrapping paper or wallpaper tear out (do not cut) individual flowers, fruit, leaves or whatever.

Paste a selection of these, overlapping one slightly with another, over the rest of the screen. Work from the edge inwards and allow some pieces to overlap the 'marble' container.

When dry, in order to make the decoration appear more three-dimensional and as though it were hand-painted, paint shadows in blue-grey gouache on the fake vase, beneath the flowers, fruit, etc, which appear to overlap the 'container' and round the lower edges of the central pieces (see detail below).

Once the paint is dry, apply a coat of oil glaze. This is absorbed by the torn paper edges in particular and helps to heighten the antique, three-dimensional quality of the decoration. When this is dry, apply one or more coats of semi-gloss varnish, allowing each to dry before applying the next.

With a jigsaw cut round the outline of the screen and smooth any rough edges with fine sandpaper/glasspaper. Also cut out a triangle of board to attach to the back with a couple of metal hinges; this supports the screen.

After applying a coat of white emulsion to the edge and back of the screen, use gouache paints to decorate them in sympathetic colours. Seal them with a coat of varnish.

Lamp

EQUIPMENT AND MATERIALS

Several lengths of wood approx. 4cm (1½ in) square	Wire-cutters/tin-snips
Hammer and nails	Pair of pliers
Handsaw	Pair of protective gloves
Electrical wire	Materials and equipment for making pulp (see page 25)
Plastic or rubber tubing	
Masking tape	PVA/white glue
Metal lamp fittings and glass globes	Fine sandpaper/glasspaper
	White emulsion paint
Screwdriver and screws (for lamps)	Brushes
	Acrylic paints, oil pastels, etc
Chickenwire	Matt varnish

METHOD This lamp is about 1m (3½ ft) high and even Louise Vergette admits that it is a lengthy and fairly complex project.

Since large quantities of paper pulp cannot safely be supported by chickenwire alone, you have to begin by constructing a rough framework from wood. You need, for instance, one long piece for the neck and spine of the figure, a cross piece for the shoulders, two pieces of wood almost at right angles to each other for an arm; a cross piece for the hips, and a long piece for each leg which goes down to join a solid, irregularly shaped construction for the base. From the base one piece of wood also projects upwards from one side to support the jug-lamp.

Once the wooden framework is reasonably stable, thread two lengths of electrical wire through plastic or rubber tubing for protection. Wire up the two metal light fittings and screw one on to the end of the wooden frame where the raised hand will be and one to where the top of the jug will be.

With masking tape secure both lengths of wiring down the frame into the base so that they can emerge from the back.

From various lengths of chickenwire form the head with its hair, the body, arms and legs, a pair of wings on her back, plus the base, the jug and the protruding log. Shaping the chickenwire is a tricky process requiring time and patience. Turn any protruding spikes of wire inwards with the pliers.

When the shape seems reasonably satisfactory, make sufficient coarse paper pulp with PVA/white glue (not wallpaper paste) to cover the whole chickenwire frame in one layer. The pulp should be dryish and sticky. Louise Vergette applies the pulp straight on to the wire,

but you can, if you prefer, paste on a layer of paper pieces first. Apply the pulp in small handfuls, a bit at a time, then smooth the surface roughly and leave to dry.

Coat the pulp with diluted PVA/white glue to strengthen the structure. When that is dry, apply the next layer of pulp, shaping the contours of the sculpture and base as you proceed. Leave it to dry thoroughly before painting on another coat of diluted PVA/white glue.

Continue adding layers in this manner until the final coating, which must be of very fine pulp.

The drapery is then created from chickenwire covered in a layer of pasted newspaper pieces, which is in turn coated in very fine pulp. Smooth the surface of the sculpture with fine sandpaper/glasspaper.

The leaves on the log are cut from matt green plastic-coated material; they are glued to wire stalks, which are in turn glued into the final layer of damp pulp with PVA/white glue. If you forget to do this at the right moment, simply add a small quantity of fine pulp to the junction of the wire with the log.

The lizard is shaped freehand from fine pulp.

Cut a piece of cardboard to fill the bottom of the base and, before you secure it in place with PVA/white glue and masking tape, remember to make a hole in the back of the base and feed the wiring through it. Cover the base with a layer of fine pulp.

Allow at least four weeks for the whole structure to dry out before priming it with a coat of white emulsion paint. Louise Vergette then uses a mixture of paints, including acrylics and oil pastels, to colour her lamp. A coat of matt varnish adds protection.

Sunray mirror

EQUIPMENT AND MATERIALS

Mounting card or card-
   board

Flexible card

Scissors and craft knife

Pencil or felt pen

Masking tape

Materials and equipment
   for making pulp (see
   page 25)

Mixing bowls

Plaster of Paris/gypsum

Water

Palette knife (optional)

Brushes

Gouache paints

Metallic powder paint

Semi-gloss varnish

Mirror

PVA/white glue

METHOD Make an appropriate quantity of paper pulp for the size of mirror you require.

Cut a circle from a sheet of cardboard/card and cut a hole in the centre to hold the mirror. Using 1cm (½in) strips of flexible card, encircle both the outer and inner rims and fix these upright 'walls' firmly in place with masking tape.

Pour the pulp on to the cardboard base until it reaches the top of the encircling rims. Press the pulp down firmly, fill in any uneven patches and smooth the surface with a palette knife. Leave to dry for a week or so in a warm place.

Make a thick, creamy mix of plaster/gypsum with water in a mixing bowl, pour this in rays round the inner rim and then shape it more precisely with a palette knife or your fingers.

Once the plaster/gypsum is dry, Julie Howells creates an intricate patchwork pattern in gouache paints in three or more layers, often using a dotted pointillist technique on the final layer. The sun's rays are covered in several layers of metallic powder paint and the whole sealed with varnish. The mirror is cut to size and secured in place with PVA/white glue to the back of the frame.

The two bowls are made from pulp shaped on conical moulds and each is supported by three balls of pulp.

JULIE HOWELLS

Gargoyle

EQUIPMENT AND MATERIALS

Shredded scrap paper, newspapers, etc

Vat or dustbin of hot water

Mixer-blender

PVA/white glue

Materials and equipment for making paper (see page 34) or shop-bought handmade paper

2 sheets of plywood

Modelling clay

Kitchen knives, sculpting tools, etc

Soft soap or washing-up liquid

4 planks of wood

Strong adhesive tape or parcel tape

Large container of water

Plaster of Paris/gypsum

Wooden stirring implement

Spoon

Wooden spatula

Sponge

Sheet of chipboard or medium-density fibreboard (MDF)

Jigsaw or hacksaw

Brushes

White emulsion paint

Brass-rubbing sticks, acrylic paints, wax crayons, wax-based gold paint, etc

Spray can of semi-gloss varnish

METHOD Since Emma Halsall's gargoyle, as she calls it, is about 91.5cm (3ft) in length and many of her other creations are fairly large, she obtains shredded scrap paper in bulk from the local council. After checking that no plastic is mixed in with it, the paper is put into a large container of hot water and left to soak for several hours. Then it is blended into pulp in a commercial mixer-blender and only a substantial quantity of PVA/white glue is added – nothing else. (Quantities are inevitably a matter of trial and error or, as in Emma's case, experience.) Make some of the pulp into sheets of paper (see page 34).

Meanwhile, on a large board, shape modelling clay by hand into a rough gargoyle shape and leave it to set for about a day until it is leathery hard. Then sculpt in details with kitchen knives or other implements. Coat the carved clay with soft soap or washing-up liquid (not petroleum jelly), especially in any nooks and crannies.

Using planks of wood secured at the corners with strong tape, build a 'retaining wall' round the clay sculpture; fill any gaps in the 'wall' with clay. Check that the top of the 'wall' is at least 2.5cm (1in) higher than the top of the clay sculpture. (If the plaster mould you are about to make is too thin, it will break.) Cover the insides of the 'wall' with soft soap or washing-up liquid.

Fill a large container with water and pour in plaster of Paris/gypsum powder until a peak appears above the surface. Leave it for one minute so that any air bubbles are evacuated and then stir the mixture gently with a wooden implement – do not whisk. The mixture will begin to give off warmth as it 'goes off', i.e. is ready to use. Spoon some of the mixture over the details in the sculpture before steadily pouring on the rest until it almost reaches the top of the 'retaining wall'.

When the plaster/gypsum feels cold, it should be set, but leave it a while longer to be on the safe side. Cover the area of plaster/gypsum with another large board and carefully turn the whole 'sandwich' of board, plaster/gypsum, clay and base board upside down.

Ease the planks away from the edge of the mould and gently remove the clay, using a wooden spatula or similar to extract the fiddly bits. Take care not to damage the new mould.

Line the inside of the mould with a slightly dampened sheet of handmade paper, easing it into the crannies with a sponge. In the same way add a second layer of paper. Then squeeze a handful of pulp to remove the water and press it into the mould with your fingertips. Once several handfuls have been applied, press the pulp down with a sponge to compact it and remove excess moisture. Continue to fill the mould in this manner until the pulp spreads over the edge of the mould. Put it somewhere warm and airy until the pulp is only slightly damp and adheres together – it must not be totally dry or it will stick to the mould.

Turn the mould upside down on a clean board and very gently ease the pulp sculpture out all the way round – use a wooden spatula, if necessary. Leave until the pulp is completely dry.

To strengthen the gargoyle, outline its shape with a pencil on to a sheet of chipboard or MDF and cut this out with a saw. Coat both the flat back of the gargoyle and one face of the board with PVA/white glue and stick them together. When the glue is dry, cover the join and board edges neatly with a layer of paper pulp, and leave to dry.

Coat the entire gargoyle with white emulsion. Once that is dry, decorate it as you will – brass-rubbing sticks are particularly effective, as are sponged on watercolours. Finally spray on a coat of semi-gloss varnish.

Cupboard and shelves

Planks of wood approx
  1cm (½in) thick.
Backing board approx
  0.5cm (¼in) thick or
  sheets of corrugated
  cardboard
Tape measure and pencil
Handsaw
Craft knife
Hammer and nails
PVA/white glue
Masking tape
Gummed paper tape

Newspapers, etc
Bowl of wallpaper paste
Rigid poker wire and
  wire-cutters/tin-snips
White emulsion paint
Brushes
Gouache paints
Waterproof black ink
Metal hinges and pins (for
  cupboard)
Gloss polyurethane
  varnish

METHOD Jeanette Orrell prefers to recycle materials whenever possible, so the frames of her cupboard and shelves are made from driftwood. However, they can equally well be made of two layers of cardboard stuck together with PVA/white glue and masking tape; once the glue is dry, the masking tape should be replaced by gummed paper tape.

For the shelves, cut a backing board from wood or cardboard approximately 84cm (33in) high × 30.5cm (12in) wide and with a saw or craft knife round one end to a semi-circle, leaving 61cm (24in) of straight sides below.

Cut two rectangles for the sides, each 61cm × 12.5cm (24in × 5in), and four shelves each 30.5cm × 12.5cm (12in × 5in). If you are using wood, nail the pieces together. If the frame is of cardboard, secure the pieces with PVA/white glue and masking tape, replacing the latter with gummed paper tape once the glue is dry. Then paint the unit with diluted white glue to prevent the cardboard warping. Cover the whole construction with three layers of pasted paper pieces and leave to dry.

Cut a bird or other appealing shape from cardboard and affix a short length of rigid wire both to the bottom of the bird and to the back of the shelves using PVA/white glue and masking tape. When the glue is dry, cover the bird with three layers of pasted paper pieces and the top of the back of the shelves with two layers. Leave to dry.

Coat the shelves and the bird with two layers of emulsion paint. When they are dry, draw your design in pencil, paint on the background and foreground colours, and then outline the design in ink. Seal with one or more coats of gloss polyurethane varnish.

With the proviso that wood makes a stronger frame on which to hang a door, the cupboard is made using the same techniques as the shelves. The back panel is, of course, shaped differently at the top and, to fit this shape, the side panels are curved into a quarter circle at the top.

Complete the shelves and door up to the stage where they are ready to varnish. Secure the two hinges to the inside of the door and to the front surface of the shelf upright with both PVA/white glue and nails or pins. Finally give the inside and outside of the cupboard one or more coats of varnish.

If you are not good at drawing, use black-and-white photocopies coloured with crayons or paint

Clock and mirrors

EQUIPMENT AND MATERIALS

For clock:

Chickenwire

Wire-cutters/tin-snips

Pair of pliers

Newspapers

Bowl of wallpaper paste

Pencil and metal ruler

A4-size black-and-white
  photocopies

Poster paints, gouache, etc

Brushes

Semi-gloss varnish

Battery-powered or
  quartz clock mechanism

For mirrors:

As above plus

Mirror

Plastic sheeting

Masking tape

PVA/white glue

METHOD Roll out a length of chickenwire and cut out a square the same as the width of the roll. With pliers tuck in the spiky wire ends and then bend the chickenwire into folds. For the tassel bend a small, loose roll of chickenwire to shape and attach it by its raw edge.

Cover both sides of the wire with one layer of pasted pieces of newspaper.

On one or more sheets of plain A4 paper draw your own design to photocopy, or photocopy images from books. Colour the photocopies and, when dry, tear each into four pieces. Paste the pieces in a random patchwork over the front and back of the frame.

On a small square of plain paper draw out and paint a clock face; glue this to the centre of the frame. Make a small hole in the centre of the face to accommodate the clock hands and, before attaching the clock mechanism, paint the whole frame with a coat of semi-gloss varnish.

The mirrors are made in similar fashion by folding in the edges of a chickenwire square or rectangle by about 1cm (½in) as a 'hem' and then, having made 4cm (1½in) cuts bisecting the corners, fold the edges another 4cm (1½in) all round. For the lower mirror in the picture attach a hemmed triangle of chickenwire by one raw edge and add a roll shaped like a tassel. Then cut a hole of appropriate shape in the centre to house the mirror; fold in the spiky edges. Cover the frame with one layer of pasted newspaper pieces and a layer of painted photocopies (see above). With PVA/white glue secure the mirror to the back of the frame. Then cover the back with a sheet of plastic (to protect the mirror) affixed with masking tape, and cover this with two layers of pasted newspaper pieces plus a layer of coloured photocopies. When dry, seal the whole with semi-gloss varnish.

Trinket cupboard, hand mirror and box

EQUIPMENT AND MATERIALS

Materials and equipment for making a plaster mould (see page 27)	Brushes
Soft soap or washing-up liquid	Acrylic, gouache or powder paints
Materials and equipment for making pulp (see page 25)	Semi-gloss varnish
	Modelling clay (optional)
Fine sawdust (optional filler for pulp)	Kitchen knives, sculpting implements, etc
Mirror	Gold paint
PVA/white glue	Hacksaw or jigsaw
White emulsion paint	Masking tape
	Metal hinges, door catch and pins (for cupboard)
	Small hammer

METHOD The basic components of all three objects shown opposite are sheets of paper pulp just under 0.5cm (¼in) thick.

The hand mirror is the simplest to start with. First of all make a shallow plaster/gypsum mould, following the directions given on page 27. It must be triangular in shape with rounded corners and sealed with a coating of soft soap or washing-up liquid.

Make a quantity of paper pulp, following the recipe on page 25, but containing more PVA/white glue than wallpaper paste and, if you wish, fine sawdust instead of ground chalk/whiting as the filler. The aim is for the resulting sheet of pulp to be dense and rigid.

Pour off any surplus water from the pulp (ideally there should be none) and tip it into the prepared mould until the pulp is about 0.5cm (¼in) deep.

To the centre of the triangular sheet of dried pulp affix a square mirror with PVA/white glue. When that is dry, build up fingerfuls of dryish pulp round the edge of the mirror and the edge of the frame, pinching it into shape.

Once the edges are dry, apply a coat of white emulsion and then five thin coats of paint, graduated to darker shades round the edges.

Sue Sanders casts her ornamental shells, starfish and nodules in plaster in a series of plaster moulds protected with a coating of soft soap or washing-up liquid, but you can, if you prefer, sculpt them in modelling clay. When dry, they are coated in emulsion and then glued to the frame. A coat of gold paint is then applied. If any paint, etc, strays on to the mirror, it can be removed delicately with the tip of a scalpel.

The box is made from six sheets of pulp. When the four sheets which form the sides are dry, cut an irregular line horizontally through them with a jigsaw. Make sure these halves are correctly matched when you glue the pieces together. Until the glue is dry, secure the joins with masking tape, then remove it. Prime, decorate and finally varnish the box as you did the mirror.

The components of the trinket cupboard are also sheets of pulp. If the pulp is dense enough, all the flat parts – the back, sides, roof, doors, shelves and angled feet – can be cut with a fine hacksaw or jigsaw from a single large sheet. Otherwise each piece will have to be shaped individually in a plaster mould (see above). In either case, the curved brackets are best shaped from pulp in a plaster mould, although it is possible to shape them freehand. The components are stuck together with PVA/white glue, secured temporarily by masking tape until the glue is dry. After removing the tape, the cupboard is primed with emulsion, painted, varnished and ornamented in the same manner as the mirror. Finally the hinges and door catch are pinned in place.

Puppet theatre

EQUIPMENT AND MATERIALS

For theatre:

Smooth cardboard with corrugated interior

Pencil and metal ruler

Craft knife

PVA/white glue

Masking tape

Gummed paper tape

Newspapers

Bowl of wallpaper paste

White emulsion paint

Brushes

Gouache paints

Waterproof black ink

Gloss polyurethane varnish

Black insulating tape

Red velvet (for front curtains)

Gold string (for curtain ties)

Black felt (for back curtain)

For glove puppet:

Modelling plastic

Petroleum jelly

Newspapers

Bowl of wallpaper paste

Scalpel

PVA/white glue

Masking tape

Gummed paper tape

White emulsion paint

Brushes

Gouache paints

Gloss polyurethane varnish

Red material

Scissors

Needle and thread

Gold braid

METHOD The base of the theatre is a solid box approximately 61cm × 30.5cm × 61cm (24in × 12in × 24in), cut from cardboard using the techniques described on page 28. Cover the base with three layers of pasted pieces of newspaper before joining it to the superstructure.

The superstructure, also of cardboard, is approximately 56cm wide × 25.5cm deep × 76.5cm high (22in × 10in × 30in). The whole of the front of the proscenium arch, including the curtain pelmet and 'footlights', is cut out all in one piece. There are two side pieces approximately 61cm high × 25.5cm wide (24in × 10in), and a strip of 56cm × 7.5cm (22in × 3in) joining the tops of the two side pieces at the back. Join all these pieces using the same method as for the base, and cover inside and out with three layers of pasted paper pieces.

Secure the superstructure to the base in the same manner and cover the joins with two layers of pasted paper strips. Cover everything in a coat of white emulsion. When that is dry, outline the decorative patterns in pencil, paint them in, outline them in ink and finally coat the theatre in varnish.

Secure the curtains of gathered red velvet to the back of the arch with insulating tape or similar. The black back curtain is in one piece, but has a slit cut in the middle to allow puppets through; this, too, is secured with tape to the inside of the back cross piece.

The crowned head of the puppet king is shaped first in modelling plastic. When it looks convincing, cover the mould with petroleum jelly and apply five layers of small pasted paper pieces. When these are dry, cut round the rim of the crown with a scalpel and remove it. Then make a vertical cut just behind each ear and remove the two halves. Immediately glue the three pieces together with PVA/white glue and masking tape. Replace the latter with gummed paper tape when the glue is dry.

After a coat of emulsion, paint the head using gouache colours and waterproof ink for the lines. Two coats of gloss varnish seal and protect the head.

Fashion the glove from red fabric and attach it to the head by turning the glove inside out and sewing repeatedly round the fabric neck and through the head. Finally, trim it with gold braid.

MARION ELLIOT AND MARIE GREGORY

Helmet, hat and crombie

EQUIPMENT AND MATERIALS

Balloon (for helmet)

Bowl as mould (for hat
  and crombie)

Newspapers, etc

Bowl of wallpaper paste

Pliable cardboard or card

Masking tape

Modelling plastic or clay

Pencil

Craft knife

White emulsion paint

Brushes

Gouache and gold paints

Tartan wrapping paper

Semi-gloss and gloss
  varnish

Tissue paper

METHOD For Marion Elliot's intergalactic helmet, follow the directions given on page 17 on how to mould pasted paper on a balloon. Put on at least eight layers and set aside to dry.

To make the spikes, roll strips of cardboard or card into cones and tape them to the helmet with masking tape. Strengthen the joins with tiny strips of modelling plastic or clay and cover the whole area with three layers of pasted paper pieces.

When the helmet in dry, cut two eye holes with a craft knife and neaten the rims by pasting on small strips of paper. Set aside to dry. Paint the helmet with white emulsion inside and out, and, when that is dry, decorate it in lively colours and false eyes. Seal the helmet with a coat of semi-gloss varnish.

To make Marie Gregory's hat and crombie choose a mixing bowl mould that will fit easily on your head, allowing for the fact that pasted paper shrinks as it dries. Following the directions on page 13 for layering paper on an existing mould, build up eight layers of pasted paper pieces. Flatten the crown of the crombie by gently pressing the damp paper on to a flat surface and set aside to dry.

Add a flat rim to either hat by following the directions on page 19. Soften the shape of the brims by manipulating the damp cardboard/card and layers of pasted paper.

Leave both creations to dry before covering the crombie with a layer of tartan wrapping paper and a coat of gloss varnish, while the hat is covered with several layers of pasted crumpled pink tissue paper tinted with watery gouache paints. The flower stem is created from rolled tissue paper and the flower head of cardboard or card covered in more tissue paper. Glue the flower to the hat and, if you wish, seal it with spray matt varnish.

Finally pray for fine weather.

Satyr, sphinx and Minotaur icons

EQUIPMENT AND MATERIALS

Cardboard	Materials and equipment
Pencil and metal ruler	for making pulp (see
Scalpel	page 25) or modelling
PVA/white glue	plastic
Brush	White emulsion paint
Masking tape	Paint brushes
Gummed paper tape	Gouache paints
Newspapers	Waterproof black ink
Bowl of wallpaper paste	Gloss varnish

METHOD The techniques used in making the sphinx are almost precisely the same as for the other two.

With pencil and ruler mark on cardboard the six pieces for the solid box base, cut them out with a scalpel and secure the joins with PVA/white glue and strips of masking tape. Replace the latter with gummed paper tape for strength once the glue is dry. Cover the base with two layers of pasted paper pieces.

Next mark out on cardboard the proscenium arch, pointed cornice and star as one piece, plus two side pieces, a back sheet, and a rectangle which will form a flat roof behind the cornice. Cut them out carefully and join in the manner described above.

Mould the raised edge and plaque on the cornice (or any other feature you wish to add) from pulp or modelling plastic and then cover all the surfaces with two layers of pasted paper pieces.

When these are dry, affix the superstructure to the centre of the base with PVA/white glue, masking tape and then gummed paper tape. When dry, cover the joins with a layer of pasted paper pieces. Leave to dry before painting everything with white emulsion, outlining the pattern in pencil, and decorating in gouache and ink.

Draw the sphinx's outline, including two tabs beneath her legs, on cardboard and cut it out. Cover her in a layer of small pasted paper pieces, model her bulging legs in pulp or plastic, and then apply another layer of pasted paper pieces. Once dry, paint with a coat of emulsion. When that is dry, draw her form and features in pencil, paint them in gouache and outline them in ink. With a scalpel, cut two slits for the tabs in the base, put PVA/white glue on the tabs and on the bottom edge of the sphinx, and slot her into place. A tiny roll of modelling plastic running along the join behind the sphinx helps to keep her in place.

Finally paint everything with one or more coats of varnish.

MARION ELLIOT

Sphinx

...nigmatic, the mysterious, Solar Power.

MINOTAUR - the Savage Passions of Nature.

take that!

My family dog and other animals

EQUIPMENT AND MATERIALS

Fine-gauge chickenwire	White emulsion paint
Wire-cutters/tin-snips	Brushes
Pair of pliers	Poster paints or similar
Protective gloves	Coarse nylon string,
Newspapers, etc	various colours
Bowl of wallpaper paste	Scissors
PVA/white glue	Fine sandpaper/glasspaper
Coarse sewing needle	Matt varnish

METHOD The lifesize dog opposite (a portrait of a beloved family pet now departed) plus the smaller horse, cow and sheep above are all created from a chickenwire armature covered with up to eight layers of pasted paper pieces, using the techniques described on page 30.

The horse's mane and tail are devised from remnants of an old fancy-dress nylon wig. However, as in the case of the cow's tail, they can equally well be made from unravelled nylon string attached with PVA/white glue.

As an alternative, the sheep, a simple, solid shape with or without its base, can be made from paper pulp in a plaster mould (see page 27).

Whether they are ornaments for the home, set around a Christmas crib in church or are part of a toy farm-yard, such animals have a naïve charm.

Christmas tree decorations

EQUIPMENT AND MATERIALS

Cardboard

Pencil or felt-tip pen

Craft knife and scalpel

Red plastic-coated wire

Masking tape

Newspapers, etc

Bowl of wallpaper paste

White emulsion paint

Waterproof black felt-tip
  pen or ink

Brushes

Gouache paints

Ribbon

Materials and equipment
  for making pulp (see
  page 25)

Semi-gloss varnish

METHOD Traditional glass baubles (which could easily have been made from paper pulp coated with pearlized and metallic paints) provide an effective foil for Jeanette Orrell's cardboard folk art decorations and Melanie Williams's mustachioed Edwardian.

Having drawn a variety of shapes on a sheet of cardboard, Jeanette cuts them out with a scalpel or craft knife. A small loop of red wire is attached to the top of each with masking tape before the cardboard is covered with several layers of pasted paper pieces. When the paper is dry, a coat of white emulsion is applied to both sides. Once that is dry, the outline and any patterns are marked on in black ink and filled in with translucent shades of gouache paint. A length of silk ribbon is threaded through each loop to hang the decoration on the tree.

The lone portrait of a man with a moustache – one of a series loosely depicting Melanie's friends – makes a novel conversation piece. Cut out a small circle of cardboard and, on top of it, mould paper pulp freehand into the desired shape. (To make a large number of such decorations you could easily create a trayful of plaster moulds – see page 27.) With the aid of a scalpel, the end of a short piece of red wire for a loop was inserted through a tiny hole in the cardboard and damp pulp. When the paper is dry, a coat of white emulsion is painted on. When that too is dry, use gouache paints to create the decoration of your choice and finally seal the bauble with semi-gloss varnish.

JEANETTE ORRELL AND MELANIE WILLIAMS

Dolls

EQUIPMENT AND MATERIALS

Newspapers, etc	Scissors
Bowl of wallpaper paste	Kapok stuffing
PVA/white glue	Needle and thread
Materials and equipment for making pulp (see page 25)	Paints
	Brushes
	Semi-gloss varnish
Dressmaking pin	Material and button (for
Calico (for body)	skirt)

METHOD The arms and legs can be formed from pulp, but Melanie Williams prefers to make them by rolling pasted newspaper strips of appropriate width into tight tubes. Round off the ends of them with tiny pieces of pasted paper and set aside to dry.

To create a smooth doll's head, roll a good dollop of dryish, sticky pulp between the palms of your hands to form a perfect sphere and leave it to dry for several days.

For the neck, roll a narrow strip of pasted newspaper into a tight tube. When it is dry, embed the blunt head of a dressmaking pin into one end with a tiny blob of PVA/white glue and the pointed end with glue into the pulp head.

Melanie likes her dolls to have flexible bodies, so she makes them of fabric cut in an hour-glass shape, stuffed with kapok and painted with mocks frills, etc. However, the body can be shaped freehand from pulp, if you prefer.

Coat the head, neck, arms and legs in white emulsion before painting the features and accessories. Two coats of semi-gloss varnish are recommended to protect the head and limbs.

As you sew up the top and bottom of the stuffed body with a coarse needle and strong thread, attach the limbs and neck by stitching through them too. For the wrap-round skirt a small rectangle of material is gathered on one long side and a waistband is sewn over it. A tiny decorative button is attached to the centre front. Hem the skirt and then, on the under side of the waistband, stitch the skirt to the body.

Dinosaurs

EQUIPMENT AND MATERIALS

Lengths of wood approx
  61cm × 5cm (24in × 2in)

Handsaw

Hammer and nails

Newspapers

Masking tape

Bowl of wallpaper paste

Latex (liquid rubber)

Brushes

Acrylic paints

PVA/white glue

METHOD All three dinosaurs – the long-necked Diplodocus, the spiky green Triceratops, and the Tyrannosaurus Rex – are all made in the same way, though their forms, of course, vary.

When his young son developed an interest in dinosaurs, Jean-Marc Faure made a couple of small ones to amuse him. Then he found he enjoyed making them, and – like Topsy and indeed, the little boy – they 'just growed'.

A simple, rough but sturdy skeleton of wood is constructed, on to which crumpled newspaper is tightly bound with masking tape. Further layers are added until a satisfactory form is achieved. Then apply a smooth layer of pasted paper pieces.

Once that is dry, paint the whole dinosaur with one or more coats of latex, allowing each to dry before applying the next.

Paint the dinosaur in appropriate acrylic colours and, when dry, apply one or more protective coats of diluted PVA/white glue.

JEAN-MARC FAURE

Toys

EQUIPMENT AND MATERIALS

Battered or secondhand self-winding mechanical cars, etc	Newspapers
	Bowl of wallpaper paste
Chickenwire	Black and red plastic-coated paper
Wire-cutters/tin-snips	Acrylic paints
Pair of pliers	Scalpel
Fine reel wire	PVA/white glue

METHOD When children grow tired of an old toy, this is an ingenious way of giving it a new lease of life. Even adults find these mechanized insects amusing.

Cut a rough circle of chickenwire and bend it into a dome. Curve the edge round the under side of the original mechanized toy and fix the chickenwire in place underneath with fine reel wire, taking care not to impede the self-winding mechanism and any wheels, etc. Use pliers to tuck any spiky wire ends safely away.

Cover the chickenwire armature with at least five layers of pasted paper pieces. When dry, attach legs and feelers cut from black plastic-coated paper to the sides and front with PVA/white glue. Then add another layer of small pasted paper pieces.

For smooth insects, decorate the body in several layers of bright acrylic paint, followed by a coat of gloss varnish.

If, on the other hand, you wish to create a furry-looking red and black bug, cut broad strips of black and red plastic-coated paper and into these make numerous vertical cuts to form a fringe. Using PVA/white glue, affix these 'fringes' in alternate overlapping bands round the body.

MIDGE LUCAS

LIST OF MAKERS

The artists listed below kindly loaned their work to be photographed for this book:

Amanda Blunden
2 Teyham Court
158 Northcote Road
London SW11 6RG

Emma Boon
New Mill House
Brampton
Carlisle CA8 2QS

Gerry Copp
School Cottage
Aisthorpe
Lincoln LN1 2SG
Tel 0522-730218

Marion Elliot
Unit 7
Omnibus Workspace Ltd
39–41 North Road
London N7 9DP
Tel 071-607-8464

Jean-Marc Faure
4 St Luke's Road
London W11 1DP
Tel 071-229-4905

Mary Fellows
Ark Interior
26 Portobello Green Arcade
281 Portobello Road
London W10 5TZ
Tel 081-960-7369

Caroline Gibbs
25 Henning Street
London SW11 3DR

Amanda Godden
2 Freshford Street
London SW18 3TF
Tel 081-947-5374

Marie Gregory
180 Broomwood Road
London SW11 6JY

Emma Halsall
2c Franche Court Road
London SW17 0JU
Tel 081-879-7673

Maureen Hamilton-Hill
56a King Henry's Road
London NW3 3RP
Tel 071-586-2344

Carol Hill
Arcadia
Cotmandene
Dorking
Surrey
Tel 0306-882017

Cas Holmes
123 York Road
Maidstone
Kent ME15 7QX

Julie Howells
35 Greenwood Road
Crowthorne
Berkshire RG11 6JS

Midge Lucas
70 Southern Drive
Loughton
Essex IG10 3BX
Tel 081-508-3358

Jennie Neame
15 Stanley Buildings
Stanley Passage
Pancras Road
London NW1 2TD

Jeanette Orrell
2 Cygnet Street
Poolstock
Wigan WN3 5BW

Paper Roses
24 Milverton Terrace
Leamington Spa
Warwickshire CV32 5BA
Tel 0926-312980

Juliette Pearce
Cross Street Studios
14 Cross Street
Hove
Sussex BN3 1AJ
Tel 0273-725321

Louise Pearson
1 Hall Cottages
Crazies Hill
Wargrave
Berkshire

Sue Sanders
10 Badger's Hill
Virginia Water
Surrey GU25 4SB
Tel 0344-844540

Nicola Sargent
14 High Street
Burcott
Leighton Buzzard
Bedfordshire LU7 0JR

Malcolm Temple
36c Trebovir Road
London SW5
Tel 071-373-6122

Pam Tipping
49 St Andrew's Road
Deal
Kent CT14 6AS

Miriam Troth
125 Seafield Road
Southbourne
Bournemouth
Dorset BH6 3JL

Louise Vergette
59 Quantock Road
Windmill Hill
Bristol BS3 4PQ
Tel 0272-292729

Katie Wallis
328 Kilburn Lane
London W9 3EF

Melanie Williams
79 Tradescant Road
London SW8 1XJ
Tel 071-735-0506